THE COMMUNITY BOOK PROJECT

Celebrating
the LITTLE
THINGS
IN Life

DONNA KOZIK, LEAD EDITOR

THERESA SCANDALE, ASSISTANT EDITOR

D1260711

For our readers... we appreciate you!

Get Your Free Gratitude Journal!

Keep a daily record of life's positive moments (big and small) with this printable gratitude journal that has room for reflecting on all the things that make your life a blessing.

- Take 60 seconds to shine a light on what's good!
- Affirmations and inspirational quotes to lift you up.
- Delivered via a colorful PDF printable.

Pick up your free gratitude journal!

www.TheGratitudeJournalProject.com

About Donna Kozik

USA Today & *Wall Street Journal* and Amazon best-selling author Donna Kozik has a passion for getting people published. Her specialty is showing people how to write a book fast and easy to use as a "big business card" for themselves and their businesses, while sharing their messages with the world.

Donna does this with her signature online program, Write a Book in a Weekend, which she has conducted nearly 100 times in the past 13 years, showing thousands of people how to get a short and powerful book done in just two days.

Get a free book planner at **www.FreeBookPlanner.com** to get started on your book today.

Need editing, proofreading, cover design or other publishing help? Check out **www.DoneForYouPublishing.com**.

Want to be a part of the next Community Book Project? Find out at **www.TheCommunityBookProject.com**.

Acknowledgments

I give great thanks to so many people for their help in putting together this edition of The Community Book Project, which was no little thing! My gratitude and appreciation go to the contributors, designers, proofreaders and more, especially my assistant editor Theresa Scandale for keeping the project on track and organized and Julaina Kleist-Corwin for leading contributor writing parties. Thank you to Teresa and Brad Castleman for constant support and cat pictures, Ruth Strebe for being my sounding board and Tara and Mike Myers for fun, inspiration and coffee conversations at summer camp. Finally, heaps of love go to all the cheerleaders in the Business Authors Association who left encouraging words in our Facebook group.

I am grateful for you!

~ Donna Kozik, Lead Editor

Note from the Editor

Welcome to this inspirational book that brings together a community of contributors who wrote brief yet compelling essays about the little things that uplift them and make life more fun and interesting.

They talk about the books that they held dear in childhood, the gardens that bring them peace and tranquility and the pets that they snuggle for comfort. There are also tales of travel and dancing in the rain, plus stories around the campfire and even a recipe for everyone's favorite comfort food: chicken soup!

The Community Book Project: Celebrating the Little Things in Life gives a nod to those people, places and memories that bring a smile even during tough times.

Join us in escaping from everyday troubles, even for a brief time, and celebrate the little things that make life good!

~ Donna Kozik

P.S. All are welcome to take part in The Community Book Project. To find out more, visit **www.TheCommunityBookProject.com**.

Meet Our Authors!

Go to this special page to meet the contributors to The Community Book Project: **www.MeetOurAuthors.com**

Contents

This Book Belongs To

Sarah-Jane Watson

"Wings have we, and as far as we can go we may find pleasure." ~Joan Lowery Nixon

"Checking it out again? We need a new card." Our librarian pulled out a blank checkout card. On the one prior, my name was written on every line front to back. It was *The Orphan Train Quartet* by Joan Lowery Nixon.

In second grade, I lived on a farm in Kansas. I loved to read. When my mom shooed me outside to play, whether up a tree or in the nearby pasture, that book was by my side. Often, I had our cats, dogs, potbellied pig and pygmy goats in tow. Together, we nestled upon a mound of hay to avoid gusty Kansas wind. I would read to them.

The plot was filled with adventure, yet the angst is what resonated with me. I wasn't an orphan, simply a child who understood loss. My family, too, was being torn apart. My dad was losing his battle with cancer. Reading *The Orphan Train Quartet* brought me joy and an escape. Its message taught me strength in times of adversity.

After Dad passed, I shared tears of grief with the characters amongst Joan's pages. I learned how to process my heart's ache and what it meant to celebrate life.

Sarah-Jane Watson is a creative professional. She lives in wild and wonderful West Virginia and is the founder of Salient Times and AdVentureSomeNess. Find out more about Sarah-Jane at **www.MeetOurAuthors.com.**

Toasty Toes

Linda Luhman

"The winter sun couldn't keep her warm. But he did." ~Nila

A lifelong Wisconsin girl, I am no stranger to cold weather. But the subzero days of 2021 have me suffering from persistently cold feet. Stay inside? Impossible. My dog is a walker and a sniffer, who only cuts it short after the mercury hits minus 15 Fahrenheit. Even if my toes do finally warm up, it is time to go back out.

Once my husband retired from his outdoor job, his boot dryer became a lonely sculpture in the bedroom corner. Tired of my lamentations, he took action. I came home from work to discover the gadget had magically relocated to our mudroom, with my outdoor footwear balanced upon it.

I was dubious, but the first moment I slipped on warm boots— heaven! A half-mile later, my toes were just as toasty as when I had geared up. I was hooked. Now my slippers take up residence on the boot dryer every time I leave the house. If I forget, I quickly regret my thoughtlessness when I return.

Much comfort and joy have resulted from this small appliance and my guy's thoughtfulness. Sadly, he needs to shop for another boot dryer; this one is now all mine!

Linda Luhman is a freelance writer and editor who currently ghostwrites in product marketing. She is always game for new projects! You can find out more about Linda at www.MeetOurAuthors.com.

The Heart of a Writer

Moira Shepard

"Keep good company, read good books, love good things and cultivate soul and body as faithfully as you can." ~Louisa May Alcott

Louisa May Alcott's *Little Women* captured my heart when I was 12, and I've read it every few years since then. With each reading, I have a deeper appreciation of Jo's commitment to writing, to telling her truth and to doing what she believes is right regardless of what other folks think.

I'm fascinated by the evolution of Jo's character as the story unfolds. She's quick-witted and passionate—qualities that lead to trouble when she's a girl and to wisdom when she matures. I admire her fierce independence and adore her wholehearted devotion to her sister Beth.

Most of all, Jo's persistence as an artist and writer inspires me. It's hard for Jo to hear Professor Bhaer criticize her sensationalistic stories, saying it would be better to sweep mud in the streets than betray her talent. Yet she bravely says, "If I can't take criticism, I'm not worth anything." Now, that's a writer with the heart of a lion.

Jo March taught me to write from my soul. To keep putting my work out there. To cultivate my soul and body as faithfully as I can. Thank you, Jo. Bless you, Louisa.

Moira Shepard helps people to develop the confidence they need to create a life they love. Find out more at **www.MeetOurAuthors.com.**

Moments and Memories

Shirley E. Kennedy

"Grandchildren are God's jewels twinkling in the sunshine of life to touch our hearts with little things." ~Shirley Kennedy

Little things bring comfort and joy, yet none touch my heart so deeply as sharing special moments with my granddaughter, Grace. The first time I held her just hours after her birth, she looked into my eyes and smiled. Time stood still as, with innate understanding, we touched each other's hearts. I knew she was special and I am captivated by her beautiful personality and ability to touch my heart with love.

It's pure magic when she laughs and runs into my arms or takes my hand and says, "Come on, Nan" when it's time to play. She shines her light and love on me so I always feel loved, wanted and special.

Life is a gift to be lived with love and happiness, and I'm blessed with both. The pure love and innocence Grace shares with me touches my heart to open it to joy, acceptance and happiness.

To my precious granddaughter, Grace, I say, "I promise to always love, protect and guide you. May we cherish the time we share and find love, acceptance and joy as we walk life's path together. Life is lived in light and darkness, so always seek the light in precious little things."

Shirley E. Kennedy writes prose and poetry with heartfelt gratitude inspired by life experiences, nature, visual and literary prompts and inner thoughts. Find out how to connect with Shirley at **www.MeetOurAuthors.com.**

Loving Seasons

Ginny Lang

"Winter is an etching, spring a watercolor, summer an oil painting and autumn a mosaic of them all." ~Stanley Horowitz

He grinned and stomped the snow from his boots. "If you had told me I'd be a grown man standing in the driveway catching snowflakes on my tongue, I'd never have believed you!"

My husband, Frank, is a native Texan, and I lived there for 30 years. The seasons in northwest Washington change fast, and the year swings from endless evenings to afternoon darkness. We were used to Texas seasons, flat as the coastal marshes, hot and wet to cold and wet and days that hold their length all year.

It didn't take long to figure out that we revel in walking in the snow under an icy full moon or that we both sniff, just a few weeks later, for the first skunk cabbage showing green and yellow through the slush.

Then comes the riot of spring color when dogwood and deep purple hydrangeas take over the roadsides.

In summer, I love telling friends down south about July fireworks that don't start until 10 p.m. because it's not dark yet.

Then fall, in shades of blood and fire like autumn in my native New England.

I didn't realize how much I missed distinct, fleeting seasons until I got them back.

Ginny Lang is a veteran management consultant, coach, trainer and facilitator to nonprofit organizations as well as an accomplished speaker and teacher. Learn more about Ginny at **www.MeetOurAuthors.com.**

Big Love From Little Things

Carole MacLean

"Sometimes the smallest things take up the most room in our heart." ~*Winnie the Pooh*

Still passionately in love, Rory and I have been married for over 30 years. Through it all, we've endured the loss of our baby girl Katherine and the delight of raising her twin sister, Margaret—a happy, healthy and successful woman. We've experienced the sorrow of parents suffering from dementia and the joy that comes from knowing we were there for them in their final years. We've lived through major career challenges and are now living the blissful life of a retirement well planned.

Over the years, we made sure the everyday minutiae of life spoke to our devotion for each other. Our great big love comes from many little things.

Small acts of kindness are the glue that keeps our love alive. Cutting grapefruit for breakfast. Emptying the dishwasher without being asked. Hiding love notes in suitcases. Replacing the toilet paper roll. These minuscule gestures are like the brush strokes of the Mona Lisa or eighth notes in Beethoven's Fifth. By themselves, nothing much, but when blended together they create a masterpiece of love.

Through the years Rory and I have navigated the largest happenings of life by filling our hearts with the smallest of things.

Carole MacLean is retired and volunteers for a local hospice by singing with the Threshold Choir. She conducts women's retreats, enjoys yoga, hiking and scrapbooking, and she blogs about self-care. Find out more about Carole at www.MeetOurAuthors.com.

COVID Challenges Have Caused Change

Patricia Jean Smithyman-Zito

"Can you remember who you were before the world told you who you should be?" ~Charles Bukowski

Conquering COVID-19, adjusting to nebulous social distancing demands of business and financial breakdown, restructuring our workplace and education systems and trying to re-create our loving family/home structures and relationships have rocked the world.

Fears of virus threats, social and political chaos and forced, fundamental life changes have caused pause. COVID survival strategies have created a rallying of champions focusing on the little things.

Struggles reveal we are not that happy, healthy or satisfied with life! We all have our stories.

I spent years living an accomplished life, unaware of needed change to be happier and healthier in my now. Despite years of professional training as a Religious Sister and teacher, I was often living in deficit, even while providing tremendous value to everyone in my life.

New strategies of self-care priorities target and transform the journey and move us to appreciate the gift of life.

Champions work to be happier and healthier, living in the now, on purpose. Blessings of COVID change.

May overflowing abundance, peace and unconditional love lead us, expand us and bless our now. Be extraordinarily kind to yourself. Change the little things from your abundant inner space, champion!

PJ Zito: wife, mom, stepmom, grandma, retired teacher, interpreter for deaf friends, musician, composer, music video creator and published author. Learn more about PJ and her offerings at **www.MeetOurAuthors.com.**

It Made Me Smile

Roberta Gold

"The little things? The little moments? They aren't little."
~Jon Kabat-Zinn

Today I took a walk, my regular daily walk, on the same path around the neighborhood. Everything felt fresh from the recent rain. I could hear the birds singing to each other as they flew by in perfect V formation. I imagined the mothers encouraging their young and praising their flying skills. It made me smile. I followed the flock until they disappeared behind a big, vibrant, puffy cloud.

The brilliant puff turned into a playful puppy quickly dissolving into a beautiful, sunlit heart. It made me smile. I felt the sun's rays dance upon my face, shielding me from the cool wind. It made me smile. Another walker spotted me, slowed down and waved as she passed on the other side of the path. It made me smile.

Today gifted me with time to take in my surroundings instead of passing through them only as a means to move my body. It resulted in my steps being lighter while my pace matched the gentle swaying of the trees arching over the route I walked. I became the voyeur of the sky, the receptacle of warmth and the amplifier of silent voices. It all made me smile.

Roberta Gold is a professional speaker, author and attitude adjustment coach. She created Laughter for the Health of It with the mission to empower everyone to have a more positive outlook. More about Roberta at **www.MeetOurAuthors.com.**

Childhood Memories

Sharon G. Teed

"Dad, even a fleeting memory of your loving smile is enough to light up my darkest days. I love you." ~Unknown

Memories of my parents come flooding back these days. I miss them.

When I was growing up, I never knew what to expect from my father. More than anything else, he loved to make people laugh.

One particular day, my mother was upset with something he had done. I don't remember what it was, but he walked away without saying a word. He rarely argued with my mother. Five minutes later, he reappeared, leaning against the kitchen door frame in one of my mom's dresses with a wig on, holding a frying pan and a spatula in his hands. He calmly said in a squeaky voice, "What's your problem?"

My mother almost rolled off her chair, she was laughing so hard. I laughed so much I had tears in my eyes. This is just one of the things he did when she was angry with him.

Daddy could always lighten the stressful situations and the nasty moods in our household. The laughter was above and beyond a simple joke. He was able to get us both to smile or laugh no matter what.

These little things make my childhood so memorable in my mind.

Sharon G. Teed loves storytelling with her writing. Editing for others has become her specialty recently. Home is Ashton Pines Retirement Community near Ottawa, Ontario, Canada. Discover more about Sharon at **www.MeetOurAuthors.com.**

Treasured Little Things

Shirley E. Kennedy

"God tests and proves us by the common occurrences of life. It is the little things which reveal the chapters of the heart."
~Ellen G. White

Sometimes the glow of life fades and I struggle on life's journey. Each time I falter, I find solace in the little things so often taken for granted. One such thing is the power of prayer, which renews my faith, hope and courage to walk life's path anew. Prayer feels like angels' wings wrapped around me in a loving hug.

As my mother lay gravely ill, I read Psalm 23 aloud to give her spiritual strength and courage. Each word renewed her faith and acceptance of God's will. With calm concern she asked if she was dying, and I said, "Yes, Mum, I think you are."

She replied, "If I die, don't cry for me, as I'm going to a better place." She held her rosary beads as we linked hands and embraced. Tears flowed as we voiced our love for each other. It was surreal, yet these would be our last words for eternity.

Those precious moments are treasured little things which bring tears to my eyes, and loving memories are imprinted on both mind and heart. Though such loss is raw and real, prayer brings light and hope to dark days.

Aim to always live without regret.

Shirley E. Kennedy writes prose and poetry with heartfelt gratitude inspired by life experiences, nature, visual and literary prompts and inner thoughts. Find out how to connect with Shirley at **www.MeetOurAuthors.com.**

Dancing in the Rain

Dixie L. Thompson

"Life is all about dancing in the rain and creating your own rainbow." ~Theras Primus

Living in the desert, it doesn't rain often. So when it does, it's a cause for celebration. It's an opportunity to go out and dance. A time to forget how I'm supposed to be acting at my age. Losing myself in the joy of motion, my neighbors are sure I've lost my mind.

The feeling of Mother Earth giving herself a shower and washing away the dust is an invitation I can't refuse. I run outside and jump and spin with joy. My hair is soon plastered to my head. I don't care if my clothes cling, revealing an old, out-of-shape body. I fling my arms out with abandon. I throw my head back and laugh. I bounce from puddle to puddle and become reenergized by Mother Nature.

When the rain ends, as it does all too soon in the desert, I smile at the sky and give thanks for another chance to play in the heavenly waterfall. Let my neighbors think what they want. Maybe one day they will join me and experience the joy I feel when dancing in the rain.

Dixie L. Thompson is a retired U.S. Army veteran, serial entrepreneur and volunteer helping others discover and reach the life they want to live. Discover more about Dixie at **www.MeetOurAuthors.com.**

Grandmother's Precious Moments

Brenda Lynn Nielsen

"If I had known how wonderful it would be to have grandchildren, I'd have had them first." ~Lois Wyse

I never imagined how delightful it would be to be a grandmother! I am having the time of my life with my young grandchildren! Confident with experience and fresh from a full night's sleep, no small child "disaster" ever flusters me. My young grandchildren are, frankly, fun to be with. I love moments of finger painting, singing, hugs and more. Their fresh approach and desire to learn and experience inspires me. Seeing the world through the curious eyes of my grandchildren has deepened my own appreciation of our natural world.

Bird-watching is a legacy of my family and a passion that I am sharing with my grandchildren. Together, we spot birds and listen to their songs. I read picture bird books with recordings of bird songs. Then we listen for the real birds' songs. We put out food and water for the birds and watch them collect materials for their nests. There is a tiny drop of pride and a sense of connection with generations of my family when I see my grandchildrens' delight in the "birdies."

Grandmother moments are full of joy, wonder and love, and I feel young and connected all over again. I should have had those grandchildren first!

Brenda Lynn Nielsen is a life and wellness coach who enjoys being a grandmother and connecting with other grandmothers. Find out how to connect with Brenda at **www.MeetOurAuthors.com.**

Daily Rituals: Nature

Lauren Julia Robinson

"It seems to me that the natural world is the greatest source of excitement, the greatest source of visual beauty, the greatest source of intellectual interest. It is the greatest source of so much in life that makes life worth living." ~David Attenborough

One of my daily rituals is being out in nature, in the garden and out on walks.

Nature makes me feel happy, peaceful and content.

My favourite time of the year is spring, when I see daffodils and bluebells and a variety of flowers blossoming and different-coloured leaves on the trees. Walking along the river and hearing its soothing, gentle flow and watching ducks swim in it. Hearing the birds, like robins, singing in the garden or when I'm out on walks. Also, hearing lambs out on the farmer's field.

I just enjoy the simple moments of being in nature.

Lauren Julia Robinson has studied health and social care. She enjoys nature and animals. Find out how to connect with Lauren at **www.MeetOurAuthors.com.**

Makeup

Tammy Atchley

"Laughter is an instant vacation." ~Milton Berle

My son, 5-year-old William, ran through the door smiling after a fun day at school. He handed me a paper from his teacher. We sat down and read it together.

"For those who missed picture day yesterday, we will be having a makeup picture day on—" My son immediately began crying, ran to his room, threw his backpack against the wall with a thud and started sobbing.

I followed him in. He looked up at me with his tear-streaked face and sobbed some more. I asked him what was wrong, and he gasped, not able to get even one word out.

Finally, he calmed down enough to say, "Mom, I just can't."

I said, "What is it, honey?"

He choked back one last sob as he said, "Mom, I can't go to makeup picture day."

I asked him, "Why?"

He answered, "The kids will laugh at me if I wear makeup to school!"

Trying unsuccessfully to hide my smile, I hugged him until he calmed down enough for me to explain. He did not have to wear lipstick to school.

Kids say the darndest things.

Tammy Atchley coaches women to build confidence in being a mom. Find out more about Tammy and her offerings at **www.MeetOurAuthors.com.**

Unexpected Sweetness

Holly Pitas

"Grandparents and grandchildren—together they create a chain of love linking the past with the future. The chain may lengthen, but it will never part." ~Unknown

Who knew that I would one day become a grandma named Yaya. It wasn't in the stars for me to have children the old-fashioned way, so I never expected the bountiful joy to come by way of my bonus sons.

Several grandchildren now add to my life, especially Ameena, as she lives near enough for us to babysit a few days a week.

Our days are filled with laughter and games. Tea parties, hide-and-seek, dancing, giving love and tummy rubs to Lucy, the dog. She helps Papa make special treats, like biscuits with butter and everything that goes with ketchup.

It's inspiring to experience her wonder with the world. We hear her squeals of delight with something as simple as a pink ball rolling across the floor or being pushed on the swing Papa built for her.

At two years old, she has her serious moments. She takes my face in her hands and strokes my cheeks. She appears to study me closely. I feel like Ameena is looking into my soul. The love overflows.

How special it is for my husband and I to savor our days of tea parties and biscuits with our sweet Ameena.

Caregiver by profession and author of *Don't Get Caught Naked: Tips for the Adult Family Home Caregiver*, Holly Pitas also specializes online as a certified emotion code/body code practitioner. More about Holly at **www.MeetOurAuthors.com.**

Connection Through Compassion

Dr. Lynne Mitchell-Pedersen

"Compassion is to look beyond your own pain, to see the pain of others." ~Yasmin Mogahed

It is April 2009. I am sitting on a park bench in Florence, Italy, taking in the splendour of the Duomo Santa Maria del Fiore in front of me. Because my arthritic hips are causing me pain, I am resting, cane at my side, while my travel companions go off to play tourist.

A heavy-set, older-looking woman limps past my bench. She wears a babushka, black boots, a long, black coat open to show black stockings and a black skirt and top underneath. She carries in one hand a cane and a heavy looking bag. In her other hand, she totes an even larger bag. We look at each other and find an instant, wordless connection. We see each other's pain.

She stops, switches her bags from one hand to the other. I know that attempt to ease discomfort. She sits down beside me and pats her knees to show me the source of her pain. I pat my hips and we both nod. Neither speaks the other's language. That moment has sealed itself in my memory, a moment of joy, celebrating universal compassion. Simple, yet profound.

Dr. Lynne Mitchell-Pedersen is a retired psychotherapist with a background in geriatric nursing. She loves to be outdoors walking, biking or cross-country skiing. Her novel, *With One Stroke*, is soon to be published. Learn more about Lynne at **www.MeetOurAuthors.com.**

Dark to Light

Julaina Kleist-Corwin

"The dark and the light, they exist side by side. Sometimes overlapping, one explaining the other. The darkened path is as illuminated as the lightened." ~Raven Davies

My alarm clock is always set a half hour before daybreak. For me, it's the perfect time to take a 3-mile walk.

The street lamps are a dim light in the dark. Bright headlights stun my eyes when a couple of cars pass me going in the opposite direction. I adjust to the blackness again. Most of my neighbors that walk for exercise aren't out this early. However, I hear shuffling footsteps and I see a moving black form heading toward me.

The figure looks hunched over, and I can't see the face. A hood drapes down from the forehead. A hoarse voice greets me. I recognize my neighbor.

"Dee, I thought you didn't like to walk in the dark."

"I don't. My face is bruised again—not something to see in daylight." She paused. "It's okay. He's gone for good."

I motion two thumbs up. She nods.

Behind her, a halo of sky is light enough to compete with the street lamps. I draw her attention to it. Soon strands of soft color brush the east. Dee and I watch the dawning of a new day together. We've emerged from the darkness to celebrate the sunrise.

Julaina Kleist-Corwin is a teacher, award-winning author and writing coach. She has three anthologies published on Amazon. She teaches five-week courses on Zoom called "5 Keys to Create Captivating Writing." Find out how to connect with Julaina at **www.MeetOurAuthors.com.**

Conversation with My Children

Dr. Apelu Poe

"Leadership never ascends from the pew to the pulpit, but invariably descends from the pulpit to the pew." ~Martin Luther King Jr.

My children would sometimes ask me, "Dad, what restaurant here in Nashville would you like to go and eat at?"

And I would say, "You know, it's funny. I, myself, would never think about that question. I was born and grew up in Samoa, South Pacific. People there would never ask that question because they take the Lord's Prayer seriously. 'Our Father…give us this day our daily bread.' That means whatever God gives you each day, that's what you eat and be thankful for."

But my children's question remains with me because it helps bring to mind a deeper reality about life. What are the little things in life that matter the most to you?

As a dad, nothing gives me greater joy than to see all my children walking in the light of God's law. The Bible says, "For the law of the Lord is perfect, reviving the soul. The decree of the Lord is sure, making wise the simple. The precepts of the Lord are right, rejoicing the heart. The commandment of the Lord is clear, enlightening the eyes. The fear of the Lord is pure, enduring forever. … And by keeping them there is great reward." Psalm 19:7-11.

Dr. Apelu Poe is a No. 1 international best-selling author who helps people live with God's time so that they may discern God's paths for their lives. Find out how to connect with Apelu at **www.MeetOurAuthors.com.**

Childhood Memories: Under African Skies

Melanie Gail Robinson

"One cannot resist the lure of Africa." ~Rudyard Kipling

In Africa, along the Limpopo and Zambezi rivers, lies a famous waterfall between Zambia and Zimbabwe, whose name is attributed to Queen Victoria. It is called Victoria Falls or referred to in local terms as "the smoke that thunders."

For the first 12 years of my life, I grew up in Zimbabwe. Zimbabwe lies in southern Africa, north of the Tropic of Capricorn.

My parents had a large farm. Many of the farms were owned by settlers who had origins in Europe, Great Britain and South Africa. Prior to the Bush War and independence.

In and around the farms, wild animals such as elephants, zebras, giraffes, hippos, leopards, lions and guinea fowls roamed.

I used to travel along dusty roads to our sprawling farmhouse with my parents. My father grew cotton, wheat, tobacco and corn.

Shona and Ndebele people helped my father on the farm. In those days people of different races got on well together, and the country could not only feed itself but its neighbours too.

My father also raised Hereford cattle, and I remember drinking lovely farm milk, jugs of cream, making our own butter and making our own strawberries-and-cream ice cream.

My mother loved cooking and baking, so I had marmalade and lemon curd from the fruit in our orchard and cakes and other goodies.

I had my own chestnut pony called Sugar Candy, who I enjoyed riding around the farm. I also had a lovely black cat called Sweep.

It was a wonderful time in my life, and it will always hold a special place in heart.

Melanie Gail Robinson is a best-selling author and TOP ambassador who lives in the United Kingdom. She loves to encourage everyone to live the life they love. You can reach her at www.MeetOurAuthors.com.

Our Pets

Emma Elizabeth Robinson

"When I look into the eyes of an animal, I do not see an animal. I see a living being. I see a friend. I feel a soul." ~A.D. Williams

Louie came into our lives. He is a soft, loving, caring and good dog. Louie has been my friend, companion and family member from the day we got him. Louie is a rescue dog.

He's so excited and energetic to go for a walk. It's a whole new adventure for him. He likes to round the family up like sheep. We take Louie for walks to help Louie get stronger because he's older now. He likes the food when I feed him.

His gentle nature shines through when we're sad. He comforts us by putting his head on our leg or arms.

J.C., our cat, came into our lives. He is a patient, mischievous, sassy, independent and good cat. J.C.'s a black cat with yellow eyes. He has a short fur coat. J.C. loves strokes on his head. He purrs when we give him chews.

J.C.'s sensible as he's street wise, knowing his surroundings. He likes to walk with us and Louie, walking in different avenues. He likes sunbathing outside and on the windowsill. He likes to explore the different avenues.

Emma Elizabeth Robinson has studied art and business. She loves nature, art and music. Emma lives in the United Kingdom. Find out more about Emma at **www.MeetOurAuthors.com.**

Little Surprises

Diane Rasmussen Lovitt

"On most days, the biggest thing you can do is a small act of kindness, decency or love." ~Cory Booker

Our children revealed their personalities by little surprises they gave us. When I was sick, our 8-year-old daughter, Jenni, quietly opened the door to my bedroom. She reached in and placed a pre-wound music box on the floor to brighten my day. Our family woke one Easter morning to find our favorite candy bars on the table. The name tag for hers was misspelled. Who brought them? No one fessed up. A month later she confessed to the trick.

Jenni's 9-and-under cross country team faced disqualification without a fourth runner, so Angela, age 6, surprised us and exclaimed, "I can run the mile." She finished last running in her school shoes on the very hilly course, but she beamed as the team picked up their ribbons.

When Chris' middle school was having a talent show, we asked if he was entering. He played the sax, keyboard and could whistle any song. He acted shy and said no. But at the show, the program included his name. He walked up to the piano, moved the chair, turned his back, knelt, put his hands on the keys backwards and played. He surprised the crowd, but he tricked us.

The siblings still grin with satisfaction when we tell those stories.

Diane Rasmussen Lovitt lives in Pleasanton, California. She writes short stories and memoirs. Find out more at **www.MeetOurAuthors.com.**

A Little Morning Ritual

Melody Juge

"I go to nature to be soothed and healed and to have my senses put in order." ~John Burroughs

Savoring my alone time in the wee hours of the morning is a precious daily ritual. My coffee is brewed and ready to be poured into my favorite mug. I grab a cashmere wrap to drape over my shoulders in anticipation of the expected damp chill of the morning air. I step out onto the porch, mug in hand, and nestle comfortably into my chair. Peaceful. No thinking. Just being. This is as close to nature as I dare to be, in the early morning darkness, here in the mountains.

I listen with lighthearted amusement to the charming sound of the birds chirping rhythmically back and forth as if communicating their plans for the day. All around there is a subtle rustling in the bushes of who knows what. There is a rich stillness in the air. Gently the sky begins to move from dark to a soft gray and slowly, little by little, the golden light of the sun peeks through the trees with a gentle glow. Enchanting. The birds start to settle down. I get a quick glimpse of a family of fawns suddenly dashing across the yard.

A beautiful preamble to the new day that has magically begun.

Melody Juge is the founder of Life Income Management™… Creating Income for Life and creator of RetirementSense™, a proprietary retirement planning process. She is an investment advisor registered with fiduciary status. Learn more about Melody and her offerings at **www.MeetOurAuthors.com.**

Mind Expansion Is Free and Fun!
Chineme Noke

"The more that you read, the more things you'll know; the more that you learn, the more places you'll go." ~Dr. Seuss

I love to read. I have always been a prolific reader and seize all opportunities to delve into the knowledge and experiences to be found within almost any type of reading matter. It was no surprise to my family, therefore, when I opted to become a lawyer. It involved reading so widely and deeply that I was in my element to be able to ingest such scholarly tomes! Whether it was legal theory (Plato, Socrates, et al.) or the intricacies of the feudal land laws in England and Wales or, indeed, the relatively dull aspects of contract law, I devoured it all, and I often marvel, fascinated, at the potentials we as human beings have—the sheer brilliance of our brain power.

My father tells of stories when, as a 4-year-old, I would get hold of books that he used as a teacher and would read and endeavour to comprehend the language within them. I recall vividly, at 5, challenging everyone with whom I met to spell Czechoslovakia as I could. I knew not where in the world that place was, but I could spell it once I had read it, and so it became my favourite party piece!

Chineme Noke is an International Literary Award winner, the founder of the Unstoppable Bizpreneurship Program and the Unstoppable Shepreneurs Group. Find out how to connect with Chineme at **www.MeetOurAuthors.com.**

Taco Night

Linda Lou Lilyquist

"The sun looks down on nothing half so good as a household laughing together over a meal." ~C. S. Lewis

My friend Gayla and I've been creating "taco night" for over 35 years. Using paper plates for the original two couples, we took the evening up a notch when three other couples joined the taco night gang. We now had real plates and Mexican figures on the table. One thing that has never changed, though, is the menu. Tacos. Made the same way every week and year after year. No beans, no rice. Just tacos! That keeps things simple.

Each taco night we station ourselves in front of a heated cast iron skillet. We fry corn tortillas, one side only, and meat seasoned with Gebhardt's chili powder is spooned in. The shells are folded over and removed from the skillet. That's it. Cheese, onions, tomatoes and lettuce are placed in order on the serving island topped off by Crystal Louisiana hot sauce.

One other thing that has been the same for 35 years—the friendships. The gang gathers at the island to build their tacos. We give thanks. Everyone heads to the table to sit, chat, tell jokes, catch up on our week. It's our favorite night of the week. Tacos and friends. Nothing compares with this simple time together.

Linda Lilyquist is a speaker, retreat leader, minister and marriage family therapist in San Diego. She loves family, friends and helping people experience life-changing transformation. Find out how to contact Linda at **www.MeetOurAuthors.com.**

A Special Time of Waiting

Katherine Wiens

"Patience is the key because when the right time comes, it will be very beautiful and totally worth the wait." ~Unknown

There has been plenty to do while we wait—setting up the nursery, appointments, laundry, shopping, resting and quiet time. We anticipate the arrival of our second grandchild any time now. I feel at peace, curious and excited. Most of all I feel thrilled as we look forward to the next few days.

Thoughts are running through my mind, such as, *When will the baby be born? Who will she look like? How heavy will she be? When can I hold her?*

I have seen ultrasound images, but they are just scans or images of her and not the real little person I can hold in my arms.

My daughter inspires me not to worry or fret but to be hopeful. She is calm as she waits for the birth of her first child. Everything is ready. She has tidied up the nursery and has packed her bag. She rests while she can.

I have been at my daughter's house for over a week, and it feels like time has stood still. This is a necessary pause as we transition from pregnancy to birth.

I am grateful to be part of this season of life.

Katherine Wiens is an online reading teacher/coach assisting elementary students to achieve reading success. More about Katherine at **www.MeetOurAuthors.com.**

Ruby's Slipper

Lynne T. Menon

"There is nothing truer in this world than the love of a dog."
~Anatole France

I rise at 5 a.m. and Ruby summons a stroke of my hand to her smooth fur coat. My loyal rescue follows me to the living room and curls up next to me on the couch. Her deep breaths reflect my meditation practice, which gives rise to space for daily intention and creativity. Om.

In the kitchen, Ruby sniffs underfoot while my Irish tea seeps. We move to the family room where my pup finds her bed by the fireplace. The flames warm her brow as they stoke my words. I savor the setting and sip my tea, basking in the quiet of the morning with Ruby nearby. I journal from my heart.

I write of Ruby's rescue. I'd not wanted another dog. Who'll train and take care of it? We went to view the Valentine's Day litter anyway. The cute brown pup waddled over, sniffed us and stole our hearts. A photo captures the day our tiny lab-pittie arrived. With her paw tucked inside one of my slippers, Ruby had found her fit.

Lynne T. Menon, M.F.A., is a memoirist and blogger. The wife and mom of two edits the California Writers Club Tri-Valley Branch website, is a freelance writer and is working on her memoir. Find out more about Lynne at **www.MeetOurAuthors.com.**

Chronic Life in 3, 2, 1

Dr. Robyn MacKillop

"Start by doing what's necessary; then do what's possible, and suddenly you are doing the impossible." ~Francis of Assisi

For those with chronic illness, finding the good in a sea of not-so-good is difficult. It's hard to recognize energetic or pain-free moments when days are mired in the opposite. Others don't understand what it's like to live with something that is constantly at odds with your body and mind. It's necessary, then, for each person to assimilate their chronic condition into the everyday so it becomes a part of functioning rather than a hindrance.

This sounds easier than it is. To adjust to having a chronic illness, one has to figure out how to live with it. Forecasting (making plans) becomes laughable, as there is no way to know how discomfort will manifest or to what level. Flexibility becomes necessary. Being able to change plans without resentment will make the day-to-day unknowns easier to manage. The person with a chronic condition is in control. Work around its limitations and live.

Some days a pair of comfortable sweats is the go-to. Other days may boil down to bingeing a favorite television show. Save your energy by having something delicious delivered, hunker down as comfortably as possible, and know the sun rises every morning.

Dr. Robyn MacKillop is an educator helping adults who didn't complete high school earn their GED. She's fiercely independent; a lover of cats, dogs, skulls, husband; pro-education; fun; and unstoppable. Find out more at **www.MeetOurAuthors.com.**

The Unconditional Love of Pets

Alberta Cotner

"An animal's eyes have the power to speak a great language."
~Martin Buber

Unconditional love can come in many forms. Although I have found none that can compare to a loyal pet. Whether it's a cat, dog, horse, etc. For me, it's my mini Australian shepherd.

Levi came into my life when I needed someone to console my spirit after a devastating loss in my life. When he looked into my eyes, he had so much love and compassion. It was like he already knew a piece of my heart was missing. I knew we had an instant bond. It was confirmed when he gave me an unexpected lick across my face.

On the tough days it's as if he already knows my heart is hurting and he's always there. Usually with a wiggle and a little attitude, which always makes me laugh and puts a smile on my face!

Levi brings so much joy, laughter and inspiration to my life. I know he loves me unconditionally.

Originally from Texas, Alberta Cotner has faced her share of challenges throughout her life. By sharing her stories and experiences, she hopes to help others navigate similar challenges. Find out more at **www.MeetOurAuthors.com.**

The Pergola Patio

Lynne T. Menon

"Home, the spot of Earth supremely blest, a dearer, sweeter spot than all the rest." ~Robert Montgomery

After moving from the East to the West Coast, we were ready to leave our temporary digs. We'd seen numerous houses, but they were all too this or not enough that. One house was different. After touring the bedrooms, kitchen, and family room, we walked out into an amazing yard. The large, pie-shaped lot was fenced in for the dog, had a studio to store our stuff and a zipline for the kids. But the best part about it was the pergola on the patio.

My husband and I had always dreamed of having a pergola, and this wooden structure, wrapped in a champagne grapevine, was manna from heaven. We pictured countless gatherings on this patio. The pergola would provide the perfect setting under which to celebrate many milestones. And a family harvest could produce delicious jam.

It's been nearly nine years since we moved into our home. We feel lucky to have celebrated a myriad of birthdays and holidays with family and friends on our patio. And the jam has been a bonus. We're so "grapeful" for our pergola patio.

Lynne T. Menon, M.F.A., is a memoirist and blogger. The wife and mom of two edits the California Writers Club Tri-Valley Branch website, is a freelance writer and is working on her memoir. Find out more about Lynne and her blog at **www.MeetOurAuthors.com.**

A Song of the Soul

Bonita Joy Yoder

"Soul music is timeless." ~Alicia Keys

Taking a morning walk along the Kaw River, I spotted a man sitting on the city's concrete bench. We made eye contact. There was something about him, with his long, dark hair and intense eyes. I said, "Hello." Next thing you know, we were deep in conversation.

He had spent the night in the park with his backpack and guitar. He picked up the guitar and started singing a beautiful song. I learned that he had written it. He shared some about his life. He planned to head south to Texas when the weather got colder but meanwhile was sleeping in this park in Lawrence, Kansas, trying to avoid additional tickets from the police for loitering.

After about 20 minutes of conversation, I went back to my early morning summer walk by the river. I wondered who was this talented man with the beautiful singing voice and deep, original lyrics? How did he end up homeless and living by the river, hitchhiking from state to state as the weather changed?

I'll probably never see him again, but I will always remember the chance encounter and being touched by his soulful song.

Bonita Joy Yoder is a "recovering" attorney, humor in business expert, emcee and edutainer who makes conferences and events more unforgettable with speaking interspersed with ventriloquism. Reach her at **www.MeetOurAuthors.com.**

Coffee Cake and Cookbooks

Brenda Lynn Nielsen

"I love to read recipe books." ~Marianne Latimer

What? Read a cookbook for fun? Are cookbooks not for finding recipes? How would one read a cookbook for pleasure? Then Marianne showed me her cookbook. Many recipes had fascinating stories or cooking wisdom. I was inspired, so for many years now, I have been collecting both recipes and stories. Amongst these is a delicious and popular coffee cake recipe that I've inherited from my grandmother. This yeast recipe contains prunes seasoned with vanilla and a dash of cinnamon and topped with a milk icing and coconut, fruit or nuts.

My grandmother was a teen living in southern Jutland during WWI. There were constant food shortages, but farmers still had a few cows and chickens. Without a coin in her pocket and wearing wooden shoes, my grandmother would walk for miles on dirt roads, past meadows and cultivated fields to visit thatched-roof farmhouses. There, she bartered for eggs, butter and milk for her family in exchange for her coffee cake. Many city dwellers did the same, so competition was keen.

Out of those hard times was born this delicious and unique recipe. I think of my grandmother's life every time that I make this coffee cake. I am reminded how tough times can birth blessings that carry through for generations.

Brenda Lynn Nielsen is a writer and life coach with a unique 360-degree perspective. In her free time, she is writing a family heritage recipe book. Learn how to contact Brenda at **www.MeetOurAuthors.com.**

Two Hearts Connected

Tammy Atchley

"I promise to handle your heart with care and treasure it with love." ~Unknown

"I love you. See you tonight!" my husband said as he kissed me and walked out the door.

Smiling, I went about my morning routine. As I thought of all the things I wanted to do that day, my thoughts kept returning to that goodbye kiss.

But then the mood was shattered as I broke a dish, my laptop stopped working and the frustration of homeschooling the kids began. I needed a break. My smile faded as I retreated to my room.

A glint of something shiny hit my eye as the light filled the room. The corners of my mouth twitched as I noticed a small box with a tiny golden bow sitting on my pillow.

I smiled again as I read the beautiful love poem my husband wrote on the card. I felt the goosebumps on my arms. I took a deep breath, opened the box, and I saw the most gorgeous necklace—two silver hearts filled with diamonds, linked together.

Somehow, he knew I would have a day like this and needed this little reminder that I am loved and the world is okay.

Tammy Atchley coaches women to build confidence in being a mom. Check out her website for a parent's guide to having conversations that matter with your kids. Find out more at **www.MeetOurAuthors.com.**

Rediscovering the Joy of Travel

Dixie L. Thompson

"I haven't been everywhere, but it's on my list." ~Susan Sontag

I joined the Army because I wanted to see the world. I had spent most of my life in Iowa and the Midwest. I got stationed in Alabama, Arizona, California, Georgia, Hawaii, Maryland, Massachusetts, Missouri, Texas, Virginia, Washington State, Germany and Korea with side trips all over the United States and Europe.

When I retired to Las Vegas, I had moved every few years and traveled every few weeks or months. I'd had enough of cars and planes. Then after several years, one of my Army buddies called. He invited me to a reunion in Houston. I had been in one place long enough. I was ready to see the world again.

I was ready to go exploring again. I reconnected with friends and classmates everywhere. I got together with them in Nashville, Louisville, New Orleans, Iowa and even hosted a reunion in Las Vegas. I started taking at least one cruise a year with other women veterans. I attended my first class reunion, our 50th, after being overseas every other time they had gotten together.

I had my wanderlust back and only took a break when the COVID epidemic hit. Look out, world. Here I come again!

Dixie L. Thompson is a retired U.S. Army veteran, serial entrepreneur and volunteer helping others discover and reach the life they want to live. Find out how to connect with Dixie at **www.MeetOurAuthors.com.**

The Man in the Mercedes

Annmarie Spiciarich

"The deeds you do may be the only sermon some persons will hear today." ~St. Francis of Assisi

My father, in our old station wagon, was not going fast enough for him. Blaring horn, flashing lights continued until Mr. Mercedes passed us, flipping the bird at my father and shouting as he did.

A few miles down the road, Mr. Mercedes was spotted on the side of the road, kicking his flat tire. All of us urged Dad to go right past him. Dad, a man of few words, said, "No, he needs help."

He pulled over as Mr. Mercedes looked mortified and more than a little frightened. My father was a large and intimidating man. Dad immediately went to work, the tire was changed, and, prior to parting, they were shaking hands whilst laughing together.

My father got back in the car. Puzzled, we asked him why he had stopped.

"It was the right thing to do."

Sometimes we learn more from what our parents do than what they say. I celebrate my parents' teachings every day in the way I conduct myself. I am eternally grateful for those life lessons. And somewhere, I am betting Mr. Mercedes also learned a great lesson in life.

Annmarie Spiciarich is a person who has lived a life of service, thanks to the inspiration of her parents. Connect with Annmarie at **www.MeetOurAuthors.com.**

My New Old Friend

Moira Shepard

"There's not a word yet for old friends who've just met."
~Jim Henson

My boyfriend calls and says, "Hey, I told a friend to shower at your place between her gigs in San Pedro and Hollywood. That's okay, right? She'll be there around 4."

I feel annoyed by his offering my hospitality without consulting me, but there's nothing to be done. It's 4 o'clock and she's knocking at my door.

"Hi," she says shyly. "I'm Kelley and you're Moira, right? Are you sure it's okay for me to do this?"

Her sweetness dissolves my irritation. I smile. "Come on in, Kelley."

She walks in wearing 2-foot-long brown clown shoes and a baggy green-and-orange Harlequin suit, topped by a curly orange wig. A bright red, painted-on smile takes up most of her face.

"Would you like coffee or water? Have a seat."

Kelley flops down on the sofa. "Water would be wonderful. Thank you!"

Two hours fly by as we talk about theater, mutual friends, life. Kelley gets showered and changed just in time to make her show. Before she leaves, we make a lunch date for next week.

The boyfriend who brought us together is ancient history, but Kelley and I remain close friends for 30 years and counting.

Moira Shepard helps people to develop the confidence they need to create a life they love. Find out more about Moira at **www.MeetOurAuthors.com.**

Cat Lady

Ginny Lang

"In ancient times cats were worshipped as gods. They have not forgotten this." ~Terry Pratchett

Nothing gives me the same kind of pleasure as watching my cats be cats.

Younger cats are action stars. You have to look up when you go into a room because they are likely to be on top of the bookcase and in motion. Back on the sofa, there they are, my girls, Suki and Mako, sleeping peacefully in front of the fire. At 3 a.m., they'll be chasing each other up and down the hall.

How about the gifts they bring, usually in your bed? "Here's a springy thing that I'm pretending is a mostly dead mouse for your pillow."

Could be worse. Could be a real dead mouse.

Cats are connoisseurs. Ozzy the Great and Powerful sat majestically in the window watching my husband, Frank, clean fish after a day on the Gulf. He preferred the roe as a treat—the caviar, if you please.

And the clowns, photo bombers. We've all watched the cat on the windowsill behind the speaker at a virtual meeting or in front walking on the keyboard to leave a string of zzzzzzz.

It's an adventure every day, living with these big personalities in those agile, little bodies. I never tire of it.

Ginny Lang is a veteran management consultant, coach, trainer and facilitator to nonprofit organizations as well as an accomplished speaker and teacher. Find out more about Ginny at **www.MeetOurAuthors.com.**

Shelter in the Storm

Joshua Grant Robinson

"The biggest adventure you can take is to live the life of your dreams." ~Oprah Winfrey

Mindfulness meditation had been recommended to me by a trusted friend. It got to the point where it was this shadow constantly following me around.

One day, I decided to face it. Being present and following along to the audio felt like I had achieved something I'd wanted for years. It was incredibly tough at first, and yet I chose it as my next big life challenge.

Each meditation felt like a workout, and the satisfaction afterward was immense. Finally, I could see a way of going back to that playful, carefree mindset I had as a child. This was me returning home.

Empowered, I thought about what I had been holding off for years. Yoga! I went to the simplest tutorial I could find on the internet. Moving breath and body together was an excellent way of staying present, and I could even become more flexible!

Between yoga and meditation, I began to feel the world open in such a soothing way. This was the answer to the storm of thoughts—to reside in this shelter. What I'd always wanted had been following me around for years. All I had to do was choose to let it in!

Joshua Grant Robinson is an actor/co-author who is currently studying at Arts College. Find out more about Joshua at **www.MeetOurAuthors.com.**

Writing To Speak

Mary Ammon MacNeith

"Speak your mind--even if your voice shakes." *~Maggie Kuhn*

Mastering the spoken word can be a bit more challenging than just writing them on paper. It's like trying to get to the moon with your voice. I found myself being invited to a speaking club filled with screenwriters, and by the second meeting as a guest, I realized I needed to learn the unique skills of speech.

It takes a village, a group of talented storytellers who can transform the written word into speech. I'm compelled to learn and compelled to share what I know through story. It's one thing to write words; it's another to speak them and speak them well so they are heard and understood. This is a skill set that I am now in the process of learning.

When I compose my words, it feels like I have a writing angel on my shoulder. As I practice speaking those words, I hope another angel will sit on my shoulder and guide my words for all to hear.

I am so very grateful for the talented writers I have encountered thus far on my journey. As I learn the art of speech, I become not just a skillful writer but a skillful speaker as well.

Mary Ammon MacNeith is an award-winning filmmaker and screenwriter and composes thoughtful ideas in her blog Shift Your Life Now. Learn how to connect with Mary at **www.MeetOurAuthors.com.**

Nourishment Served with Love

Diane Rasmussen Lovitt

"The nourishment of the body is food, while the nourishment of the soul is feeding others." ~Imam Ali

Midwestern cooks are known for overcooking meat and changing vegetables to mush. But they make buns, cinnamon rolls and desserts like experts and serve bountiful gifts.

The church and extended family communities knew that Aunt Mary made the best perfect pies—pumpkin, creamy, fruity, all with flakey crusts. I have fond memories of her and her gifts to us.

For my January birthday, I invited several girlfriends to our farm home for a slumber party. Mom had planned her day so the dough was mixed, raised, deep fried and coated with sugar in a paper bag; hot donuts timed just as we exited the school bus. My friends and I raved about those wonderful treats served with love.

My grandmother spread love through feeding the soul. She didn't have a car, lived in a small town, so she walked a quarter mile to the grocery store. One day, when my boyfriend and I were unexpected visitors, milk was all she had to offer. John accepted, even though he generally did not drink it. So each time she knew we were coming she said, "Oh John, I went to town to get you some milk." Every time, he drank in the love.

Diane Rasmussen Lovitt grew up on a Kansas farm and now lives in Pleasanton, California. She writes short stories and memoirs. Find out more about Diane at **www.MeetOurAuthors.com.**

My Search for Meaning

Karen Lynn Robinson

"If there is meaning in life at all, then there must be meaning in suffering." *~Viktor Frankl*

Have you read *Man's Search for Meaning*? Most inspiring book ever!

At 12, I overdosed on Tylenol; I was void of hope and miserable. My natural disposition is lighthearted and playful. What happened? What drove the young girl in me to overdose? Abuse.

I grew up with derogatory comments and beatings. My suffering was nothing like Dr. Frankl's in the concentration camps. Yet he shared his bread crust and encouraging words and bore witness to tears. How inspiring that, despite his suffering, he focused on little things. Attitude, words, helping another and accepting help.

Suffering is not a little thing. Little things making a difference? God winks. Dictionaries define it as "an experience so astonishing, it seems divine." God winked at me, propelling a search for my personal meaning. I realized my life has meaning when I survived a toxic overdose with no sickness.

It's a novel idea to find hope after suffering. I'm amazed when hurting people bounce back and how I have bounced back too. Suffering is a part of life. Why not find glimpses of inspiration, hope and joy? These little things and a God wink provide us personal meaning.

Little things aren't so little after all.

Karen Lynn Robinson is a licensed clinical therapist and transformation coach for career mothers desiring healing from child abuse/trauma. Heal Thrive Dream LLC is a mother-daughter company. Reach Karen at **www.MeetOurAuthors.com.**

Church Memories

Dr. Apelu Poe

"While we may not be able to control all that happens to us, we can control what happens inside us." ~Benjamin Franklin

Many people have come up to me and asked, "Who are you? And where are you originally from?"

And I would say, "I'm Dr. Apelu Poe. I'm an ordained pastor and a Torah [Hebrew] code developer. I'm originally from Samoa, South Pacific. Currently, I'm the pastor of Bethel-Woodlawn United Methodist Church in Clarksville, Tennessee."

Of course, they know that I'm the pastor at the above church. But they want to know what my church ministry does. So, I would give them a smile and say, "I help people meet their moral and spiritual needs. I help them get connected to God's mind."

And they would say, "Why do you do that? Why now in a time when the world is in crisis?"

And I would say, "Because that is my divine calling."

So I would share my story with them. Upon graduation from Malua Theological College in Samoa in December 1981, I had a divine encounter with God, just as God had called Abraham in Genesis 12:1-3. That's what brought me here to the United States.

Right now my commitment and passion are in helping people live with God's time so that they may discern God's paths for their lives.

Dr. Apelu Poe is an international best-selling author. His forthcoming book is entitled *How to Live with God's Time: Hidden Secrets of the Master's Mind*. Find out how to reach Dr. Poe at **www.MeetOurAuthors.com.**

The Joy of Grammyhood

Paula Casey Githens

"A grandmother has ears that truly listen, arms that always hold, love that's never ending and a heart that's made of gold."
~Julia Turner

Grammyhood began as a miracle of synchronicity. My first two grandsons came into the world when the busyness of middle age was behind me. I'd already enjoyed many years as a small business owner. My time was flexible, and I was healthy, strong and grateful for the opportunity to spend meaningful time with them as little angels in tiny bodies.

I rediscovered the joy of cradling them and singing songs I sang to their dads. As they grew into toddlers, we shared the joy of giggling, being silly and meeting imaginary friends in books and stories. I was able to revisit the world through their fresh, clear vision. We marveled at observing flowers as they grew, ants as they carried heavy gifts to their queens on their antennae and simply the novelty of discovery.

Most surprising was when I let go and surrendered to becoming and living in the newness of the present moment. The dormant child within me awakened to the innocence and magic of each adventure. I bask in the eternal now of each new experience as they grow. I am, indeed, blessed.

Paula Casey Githens' passion is writing inspirational articles and creating stories for her grandchildren. She draws upon her experiences as a professional prayer practitioner and spiritual mentor. Contact Paula at **www.MeetOurAuthors.com.**

First Flight

Marissa Nicole Shaw

"Only those who will risk going too far can possibly find out how far one can go." ~T.S. Eliot

My grandfather's stage name was Curly Lou Cody. He was a professional daredevil. There were pictures all over my grandparent's house of his death-defying days.

When I was 4 years old, he asked me if I wanted to go for a ride in a four-seater Cessna plane. I sat in the co-pilot seat. Granddad educated me on all the cockpit controls as we sought permission for takeoff. "Marissa, as part of the flight crew, I need your help to steer the plane," he said.

As we were about to clear the runway, he said, "Pull up on the steering wheel."

With exhilaration, I completed the task. As we reached a cruising altitude, the control tower gave us an "all clear."

"Can you teach me how to do your airplane tricks?" I asked.

"Yes, I can."

My grandpa and I pointed the nose of the airplane straight up like a rocket. Then we rolled the plane 360 degrees a few times. My granddad and I flew together every time I came to visit. The flights we took together taught me the importance of taking risks and provided me with great memories.

Marissa Nicole Shaw is a disability rights advocate, researcher, writer and health enthusiast. Find out how to reach Marissa at **www.MeetOurAuthors.com.**

They Will Never Be Gone!

Patricia Jean Smithyman-Zito

"A single act of kindness throws out roots in all directions, and the roots spring up and make new trees." ~Amelia Earhart

The back door crashed open as Eileen rushed in, eyes focused on the distant piano. Chortling about hearing a new song on the car radio, she whizzed past me to slide onto the bench. Mesmerized, I watched her magical fingers fly across the ivory as the complex, beautiful song "Alley Cat" filled my heart and our house!

That moment astounded me at age 13. Eileen heard a song and played it!

Sharing her amazing talents and unconditional love with me rooted a passion and appreciation of music that I have resourced my entire life.

Eileen! My mom's best friend and my dad's sister. The girls met at work. Teenagers who blended friendship, families and 60 years of life into a performance of love that, to me, was exceptional.

Freely sharing her gifts, my aunt impacted my life more than most will ever know. I have composed and published 30 songs, and, like Eileen, I can't read a lick of music!

My mom, segueing a vibrant 95, outlives her two loves.

Missing them, she wings up an eyebrow and utters, "They will never be gone. You're just like Eileen!"

I nonchalantly knuckle a tear from my eye, humbly whispering, "Thanks, Mom!"

PJ Zito: wife, mom, stepmom, grandma, retired teacher, interpreter for deaf friends, musician, composer, music video creator and published author. Learn more about PJ and her offerings at **www.MeetOurAuthors.com.**

Holidays Matter

Kathy Carpenter

"A thing of beauty is a joy forever." ~John Keats

Holidays matter—the celebrations, the traditions and the decorations. For my mom and me, decorating is our moment of happiness, our pockets of joy, our time together.

Mom's passion and fascination for decorating developed later in life as did mine. Mother of six kids, she didn't have the time or resources for self-expression. Given more time and space, she accumulated a huge collection of seasonal and holiday decorations.

Her grandchildren loved helping her get them out and watching her craft the displays. Awards were bestowed upon her artistry at the local fair. Twenty-something, I was oblivious to the appreciations one acquires over time. But the foundation she built fueled my desire to give due respect to each holiday.

For Mom, it's being able to celebrate the visual reminder of what each holiday represents, the sense of season. For me, it's bonding, the expression of combined creativity, texture and design. A personal reflection in a time where retailers whiz past certain holidays with a whisper so soft people don't even notice.

Real joy comes from the ability to gaze upon our displays around the house and, for a short period, appreciate the season or holiday together.

Kathy Carpenter is a writer, theatre commentator and marketing strategist bringing out the sparkle in people. Reach Kathy at **www.MeetOurAuthors.com.**

Calabash: An International Literary Festival

Melissa Rowe

"One good thing about music—when it hits, you feel no pain."
~Bob Marley

Calabash is one of my favorite holiday gathering spaces, a literary writers' festival with some of the world's best authors of African descent reading their most important works. A yearly get-together held in Treasure Beach, a small, rural, non-touristy community of down-to-earth, rural Jamaicans who opened their lives to welcome visitors wanting a simple vacation experience.

People from all walks of life come to the festival in a beautiful setting with the sea crashing behind them as they enjoy the surroundings. I especially enjoyed the food combined with the music that went all night until the sun came up.

Let me share Treasure Beach, Jamaica, in a way that you can see it with your mind's eye. Not easy, since the place is not just another spot on the map—it's a way of life. Pictures and words can do so much and no more. It's an escape from the bustle and stress of a frantic world. It's a coastline with character. The beaches are earthly with glistening dark sands and white caps often visible from the shoreline. If you are craving space to yourself, you can often find a spot where you're the only person on the beach.

Melissa Rowe is a life and anger solutions coach who supports women in supporting themselves and recognizing their strength, power and greatness from within. Find out how to connect with Melissa at **www.MeetOurAuthors.com.**

Make Time for Yourself!

Joan Powell

"Mind. Body. Soul. These are the three things self-care is all about." ~Kathy Sledge

One of the many things I didn't quite understand until I became a mom is the concept of "me time." In my single days, when my co-workers who had kids would talk about making time for themselves and self-care, I just didn't get it. How can you not make time for yourself?

Years later, when my son was born, I had the ah-ha moment. I now had to answer to another being's needs and wants, no matter what time of day. I felt like my whole existence was for the purpose of keeping my child happy, not hungry, and dry. It was hard to find even a few minutes to myself.

I've come to appreciate me time and carve out as much time for self-care as possible. I know I have to take care of myself to take care of others. I get up early in the morning before the rest of the household to exercise or sit with a cup of tea or coffee and just relax before the hustle and bustle of the morning rush begins. I enjoy the quiet. Or I take in an occasional massage or a dinner out with girlfriends. This is my me time.

Joan Powell is a freelance writer and digital marketing strategist helping entrepreneurs and small businesses build their online presence. Find out more about Joan at **www.MeetOurAuthors.com.**

Dandelion Wishes

Gwyn Goodrow

"Come, let us have some tea and continue to talk about happy things." ~Chaim Potok

Dandelions grew by the dozens in my childhood fairyland. I offered wishes for myself and my friends while blowing the dandelions. Gentle puffs of breath propelled white orbs of fluffy pappi into the air. The wind carried my hopes, and I trusted in the future to grant those wishes.

The dandelion's yellow blossoms signal the shift to springtime. More than a pretty weed growing on the lawn, dandelions provide culinary and medicinal benefits. But in my youth, dandelion wishes were whimsical diversions from farm life.

Life progressed. My childhood wishes faded from memory until Ann reintroduced me to the plant. Those blossoming flowers, green leaves and roots are valuable ingredients for dandelion tea. We strolled through the yard on warm spring days, admiring the dandelion plants while Ann shared heartening stories about my husband's life as her youngest child. Our time together was an unexpected blessing.

In the season of thanksgiving, Ann gathered her beloved pets at the Rainbow Bridge, then reunited with her husband in heaven. Perhaps she's enjoying a cup of steaming hot dandelion tea.

After the harsh and lonely winter, flowers blossom. I reminisce about my sunny days with Ann and dandelion wishes.

Gwyn Goodrow is co-founder of Cabins or Castles, where she blogs about hospitality destinations and the personal transformation benefits of journaling. Gwyn enjoys travel, creative arts and time with family and friends. Find out more about Gwyn and her blog at **www.MeetOurAuthors.com.**

I Found Waterdogs!

Cynde Canepa

"The mountains are calling, and I must go." ~John Muir

One day I was at a client's RV dealership, and I bought a motorhome. My husband and I always said we would not be that couple with a motorhome, and what do I do but bring home a motorhome.

Loren said, "I am not going to be staying in a tin box and do nothing," and he started searching online for something to do when we are in the motorhome. He ended up buying a Polaris RZR.

We use the RZR to explore the mountains a lot! One time we came upon a pond way up on the mountain, and when I looked inside the pond, there were thousands of waterdogs swimming. If you don't know, waterdogs are little amphibians.

Seeing those waterdogs reminded me of when I lived on the Cagle Ranches as a young child. I would walk down to the Umpqua River with my bucket and fill it with waterdogs. I would bring them to the farmhouse and sit on the steps, where I would play with them for hours. Then I took them back down to the river and let them go.

It truly is the little things in life that make the most precious memories.

Cynde Canepa, B.S., E.A., L.T.C., is founder of A-Z Business Services. She teaches financial safety while living an Oola balanced and growing lifestyle. Find out more about Cynde at **www.MeetOurAuthors.com.**

Pete's Coffee

Sarah-Jane Watson

"Friends are chosen family." ~Unknown

For some, a cup of coffee is simply a cup of coffee. Not me. Coffee is my longtime friend named Pete.

I met Pete in my senior year at my fifth high school. I lived by myself in a small studio apartment. Originally from Kansas, I didn't know anyone in Maine. But then I started a new job and made a friend in Winnie. She invited me to her house to meet her family, when her husband, Pete, did a sweet thing and made her a cup of coffee. Then Pete asked me, "What do you drink in your coffee?"

I answered, and he teased me about the amount of sugar I used. It became an ongoing joke between us, and one day I brought him a big bag of sugar just to see the exasperation on his face. Pete may have been sweet, but he thought coffee should taste like coffee.

I have sat around their kitchen table on countless occasions sharing the everyday joys of life and its sorrows—always with Pete's coffee in hand.

Twenty years later and Pete's coffee is still the best coffee. It's not the flavor or the type of coffee beans he uses. It's not because he holds the expertise of a barista. It's because Pete and Pete's coffee are a reminder I'll always have a home away from home.

Sarah-Jane Watson is a creative professional in wild and wonderful West Virginia with more than 17 years of experience in photography, design and marketing/advertising. Reach Sarah-Jane at www.MeetOurAuthors.com.

A Precious Resource Once Ignored

Cindy Barnard Mills

"When the well's dry, we know the worth of water." ~*Benjamin Franklin*

I grew up in an agricultural area, but I never even planted a seed. How the food got from the farm to our dinner table wasn't something I thought about.

Now we own property without city water and rely on a well. Wonderful. Pre-escrow testing showed everything was fine. No water bill. Yippee, it was free!

In the sizzling summer of 2020, the water we took for granted ceased to flow. Surely it was a pump motor or something minor. The pump was bad, but we learned the walls of the well had also collapsed. For $150 you can order a truck to deliver 150 gallons of water to your house. Who knew? We used up the first batch in two days. So we learned to conserve. Quick showers; the vegetable garden and green lawn all died.

The drilling company gave us the estimate without guarantee they would actually hit water! (Goodbye remodeled kitchen I was saving for.) Six weeks and $18,000 later we have a working well.

My appreciation for water is present with every turn of the faucet. I am grateful for the amazing earth, where the life-sustaining water bubbles up from the ground, like magic, sort of.

Cindy Barnard Mills, R. N., teaches dialysis theory and is the author of *Leader for Life*. She lives in Clovis, California, with her husband, Robert, and dogs, Otis and Fitzsimmons. Learn more about Cindy at **www.MeetOurAuthors.com.**

A Soulful Night To Remember

Bonita Joy Yoder

"Surrender to the light with a tranquil mind and a heart full of the love of God." ~White Eagle

When in Kansas City one night, I drove to nearby Unity Village. I arrived about 10 at night and wandered around the grounds. Not another soul was in sight. I walked amongst the rose gardens and water fountains before crossing the bridge that spans a pool of water. I believe if that bridge could talk, it would span the threshold of time with stories of love, romance, weddings and spiritual discourse.

I sat down at the end of the bridge. When I looked up at the lighted tower, awe and wonder filled my being. I had a sense of something beyond myself. Something greater. It was as if the whole of Presence was awakened in my soul, an inner joy.

Though no one was around, Spirit was there. I had an awakening and my heart felt open. I did not want the experience to end. Rather, I wanted to carry that awakened sense with me far and beyond. No security guards appeared. I was left alone. But not really. I was with myself, my own inner beloved. I was also with "the Beloved." Beloved with a capital B. How could I want for anything more?

Bonita Joy Yoder is a recovering attorney, humorist, humor coach, emcee and edutainer who makes conferences and events more fun and unforgettable with her ventriloquial puppet friends. Connect with Bonita at **www.MeetOurAuthors.com.**

Happy Noise

Patricia Bumpass

"If everyone started off the day singing, just think how happy they'd be." ~Lauren Myracle

I've always been shy about singing in public. The only place I'm comfortable belting out a tune is alone in my car, where it doesn't matter how you sound.

While I started filling up my car at the gas station one day, the guy at the neighboring pump stared at me. I glanced around to make sure we weren't alone in the lot and thought to myself, Why is this man staring at me? Is he some sort of pervert?

He hung up his pump and replaced his gas cap at the same time I did. Then he made his move.

"Excuse me. I'm sorry to have been staring, but I was listening to you sing."

One foot inside my car, one foot out, I glared at him, believing he must have bumped his head when he got out of his vehicle.

He continued, "Happy people sing, and I needed a little happy. Thank you."

I watched in stunned silence as he drove away. Reflecting on the conversation, I realized a stranger taught me it doesn't matter what you sound like as long as you're happy making your own kind of joyful noise.

Patricia Bumpass is a content marketer and coach. She empowers and encourages women to love themselves. Find out more about Pat at **www.MeetOurAuthors.com.**

Age with Ease and Grace

Paula Casey Githens

"Blessed are the flexible, for they will not be bent out of shape." ~Unknown

There's an old saying, "With all the - - - - in here, there must be a pony somewhere!"

We all experience challenges in our daily lives, and how we choose to view them determines how we feel. I ask myself what I can learn from a given situation, which helps, as does giving myself something else to focus on. I put myself in the other person's shoes and consider what may be going on in their life. There's always a gift when I look deeply enough.

I've trained myself to turn situations around in my mind. Over time it's become a habit, a secret to aging with ease and grace. The small things no longer get to me. If there's a last minute change of plans, I think of things I can do instead. Allowing myself to get upset doesn't solve or change a situation, and choosing to view it from a different perspective does.

I've discovered that nonresistance to change is a gift I can give myself. I live in a peaceful world.

Paula Casey Githens' passion is writing inspirational articles and creating stories for her grandchildren. She draws upon her experiences as a professional prayer practitioner and spiritual mentor. Contact Paula at **www.MeetOurAuthors.com.**

Sadie's Morning Ritual

Linda Luhman

"The silence in the morning holds lots of expectations and is more hopeful than the silence at night." ~Victoria Durnak

Sadie was 100 pounds of anxious German shepherd mix. She ate my curtains (and one flip-flop), but it was our morning ritual that I cherish the most.

I am not a morning person, tending to exit the bedroom in a fog before settling on the couch for a few minutes. Sadie always took advantage of my inactivity by ambling over and plopping her massive head into my lap for some affection.

One morning, I failed to stay upright. Concerned at my prone position, Sadie poked her snout in my face, brow wrinkled. Satisfied that I was still breathing, she bestowed a few delicate kisses to urge me on. When all she received was an outstretched hand, Sadie decided to make the most of it by pacing along the couch, facilitating a body rub. This sequence soon developed into a routine, with Sadie beelining to the sofa as soon as she saw me each morning.

After Sadie succumbed to bone cancer, these morning sessions ceased; my other dogs failed to see the value in such exertion. However, I still occasionally find myself stretching out on the couch, silently waiting for a cold nose to come my way.

Linda Luhman is a freelance writer and editor who currently ghostwrites in product marketing. She is always game for new projects! Find out how to contact Linda at **www.MeetOurAuthors.com.**

Growing Up at 30

Dena Crecy

"A daughter will follow in her mom's footsteps, so make sure to set a good example." ~Elizabeth George

My daughter is growing up to be a maturing woman and mother. God called her to motherhood at 17, and she has been slowly accepting it ever since.

From calling Mom back-to-back-to-back-to-back-to-back when no answer because she wants to tell her about something that happened to now calling one time and sending a text when no answer. From calling Mom hysterically yelling and screaming when life happens to now calling, getting a cry out and moving on to the next thing.

At the present time, she is three kids in and doing an amazing job as a single parent. There is Jaden, the oldest at 12, Kayson, 8, and Ms. Penelope, 18 months. Her children are her priority. She is actively involved in school and daycare and lets all teachers and caregivers know she cares. She plans activities for holidays, birthdays and just everyday life.

I have watched her actually use some of the advice offered and see it works. I celebrate Sydney and the woman she is becoming. It is like watching a flower that is a bud coming into bloom. Keep pouring into your children, and you will see the fruit of your labor.

Dena Crecy is a life coach who glorifies God by discipling women into their God-given purpose. Learn more about Dena at **www.MeetOurAuthors.com.**

Star-Filled Nights

Carol A. Peña

"No sight is more provocative of awe than is the night sky."
~Llewelyn Powys

Years ago, I attended a party in a rural suburb. Being from a large city, the thought of driving more than an hour one way was a bit taxing. Still, it was a much-needed break after a hectic week.

It was a clear, chilly Texas night. On the patio, small talk and music faded as I stared straight up into the star-filled night. The millions of stars were mesmerizing. I could almost feel the Earth moving on its axis as a single cloud rolled across the sky. The longer I gazed, the clearer the constellations became. It took my breath away. In the peaceful stillness of the moment, I felt the stresses of the week melt away.

I still remember the wonderment of that evening. It was not a view you get in the big city with all its tall buildings and street lights. Nor could any internet picture do the image justice.

Some years later, I left the big city. Although the commute to work is a little longer, I continue to find calming rest on clear, starry nights. For me, enjoying time with friends and family under a shimmering night sky is one of life's simple pleasures.

Carol A. Peña is a native Texan with a passion for creative writing, genealogy and adventures with Buster the Wonder-Yorkie. Find out how to connect with Carol at **www.MeetOurAuthors.com.**

The Healing Power of Music

Tracey Doctor

"Alone time is when I distance myself from the voices of the world so that I can hear my own." ~Oprah Winfrey

I relish my alone time, when I'm listening to soothing jazz saxophone music. On raining afternoons it helps me focus on whatever task is at hand. On other occasions, it completely relaxes me. Whether I am enjoying the music during a meal or while having a glass of wine, after a hectic day, jazz sets the perfect energy.

Especially when I soak in a warm, fragrant bubble bath of essential oils. Jazz creates a relaxing, soothing ambiance that I look forward to each day. Listening to the therapeutic sounds make it easy to let go of stress and meditate on future endeavors.

Many times I find myself reflecting on everything I am grateful for. I really miss the companionship of my beloved dog Benji by my side. Sadly I had to put him down a year ago. I still feel the pain from the loss of his loving and comforting presence. I cherish my memories of us snuggling and enjoying the music together.

In many ways it has become therapy for me during these uncertain, trying times. Music is a blessing that has the power to heal people of all ages and even animals.

Tracey Doctor is a holistic lifestyle coach. Her passion and purpose is helping women to find their joy. Connect with Tracey at **www.MeetOurAuthors.com.**

Stickball

Linda Lou Lilyquist

"Life gives us choices. You either grab on with both hands and just go for it, or you sit on the sidelines." ~Unknown

Each holiday we entice our grandboys, their friends, our nephews and the adults that come with them to play a game of stickball. It's just like baseball except for the stick, a 3-foot dowel with a wrapped end for the grip. The ball basket is filled with a good supply of tennis balls, and there's chalk for the scores recorded on the sidewalk. Out to the street we go. Bases are marked, teams chosen, and the pitcher takes the mound.

The fans arrange their chairs on the driveway to watch the game. One time a fan who was done watching determined to become part of the action. My 92-year-old father walked out to home plate. He arrived with his cane, which he quickly traded for the stick as we imagined him reliving a slice of his long-ago childhood.

Eying the pitcher, he assumed the stance of a much younger man and slugged that ball. As everyone cheered, the outfielders scrambled to play the hit. He made it to first base, rounded second and third with home plate in his sights.

As he scored his run, he became our uncontested MVP and brought us all home.

Linda Lou Lilyquist is a speaker, retreat leader, minister and marriage family therapist in San Diego. She loves family, friends and helping people experience life-changing transformation. Contact Linda at **www.MeetOurAuthors.com.**

Becoming a Book Lover

Anne Hunter Logue

*"There are many little ways to enlarge your child's world.
Love of books is the best of all." ~Jacqueline Kennedy Onassis*

When I was a kid, we used to have a family tradition on the weekends of taking what my father would call a "Sunday drive." I grew up in the suburbs of New Jersey, and our Sunday drives would take us to the country where life was a bit slower and simpler. I'm sure it was a welcome relief for my father after working all week. We would often stop at a local diner or country restaurant and have an ice cream soda and a sandwich or burger. We would sit at the counter on high red stools and enjoy our Sunday afternoon.

The main focus for our Sunday drives, though, was my father's interest in rummaging through antique stores and little shops looking for books. We would sift through moldy, dusty shelves, and my father would search for first editions. At the time, as a child, it did not always seem the most interesting thing to be doing to spend my time. He would bring his treasures home, and they would be in our modest home library. My love of books and the value of books was built from these excursions with my family so many years ago.

Anne Hunter Logue is a healing practitioner and children's author of *The Story of the Sun* and *I Once Had a Tiger*. Learn more about Anne at **www.MeetOurAuthors.com.**

Getting Ready for a Brilliant Day

Roberta Gold

"Give every day the chance to become the most beautiful day of your life." ~Mark Twain

Gazing through the window panes into a world full of possibilities, the day awaits me. I am able to create the day I want—sunshine or not. My attitude dictates how it will be.

Starting with closed eyes, I take a deep breath in through my nose, then slowly let it out through my mouth. In and out a few times and I am centered. I envision how I want my day to look—complete with vivid pictures of where I will be, who I will be with and what I will be doing. My face awakes and shows itself with a smile, a sparkle in my eyes and a gentle rumbling throughout my body igniting the endorphins, which fill me with an overall good sensation.

I set my intention to greet everyone I encounter with the smile I keep on me and a cheerful, welcoming hello. The best thing I discovered to ensure a good day is to help others have an equally nice day by being warm and friendly. I delight in seeing others smiling, laughing and having fun. It multiplies my joy, which guarantees my day will be as planned.

I am ready to have a brilliant day.

Roberta Gold is a professional speaker, author and attitude adjustment coach. Her mission: Empower everyone to have a more positive outlook by seeing the humor instead of the horror in our world. Find out more about Roberta and her offerings at www.MeetOurAuthors.com.

Sweet Light
Sarah-Jane Watson

"I am forever chasing light. Light turns the ordinary into the magical." ~Trent Parke

Some people geocache, bird watch or hunt for Pokémon when they are out and about. I am a seeker of light.

While attending the Hallmark Institute of Photography in Turners Falls, Massachusetts, my portrait professor, Don Ayotte, taught me about stops of light, using f-stop settings to double or half the amount of light that enters a camera. He taught me the technical terminology, then challenged my class to take on the world with a different perspective by finding stops of light in our everyday lives. From that point forward, I have done exactly that.

I enjoy seeing light everywhere. Sometimes I notice light when I am driving down the country roads of wild and wonderful West Virginia or when I am taking a walk around my garden close to sunset when light is soft, warm and sweet. Especially seeing shadows and watching as light increases the ambience by one, two, three, four stops. It allows me to see the world around me in ways I would have never seen it before. It brings me focus, peace and appreciation for the universe on the brightest of days and on the darkest of ones.

Sarah-Jane Watson is a creative professional who encourages entrepreneurs, business owners, coaches and consultants to become unstoppable in their online social media and branding presence. Learn more about Sarah-Jane at **www.MeetOurAuthors.com.**

Deep Breath, Mom

Patricia Bumpass

"I hope you find, as I did, that happiness comes from noticing and enjoying the little things in life." ~Barbara Ann Kipfer

"Your son has autism. He may never feed himself. He may never dress himself. He may never walk or talk. I'm sorry," the doctor informed me with eyes downcast.

I felt as if an unexploded grenade had landed at my feet.

From the point I strapped my then-3-year-old son into his car seat, my life as a single mom revolved around his needs. I managed his therapies and his schoolwork. I developed individualized education plans (IEPs) and attended transition meetings. When teachers and other professionals said he couldn't, I believed he could.

At one contentious meeting, it was my son who reminded me about celebrating the small things. While I explained to the professionals why he needed to be educated with his typical peers, my son took my hand and said, "Deep breath, Mom. Deep breath."

All talking stopped.

Standing up, I placed my hands on the table and said, "Let's reschedule. I'm taking my son to play in the park." I left that meeting feeling light-hearted and carefree.

Even though he's an adult now, every smile, every "Hi, Mom" reminds me, no matter the situation, it's okay to take a moment and breathe.

Patricia Bumpass is a content marketer and coach. She advocates for her adult son blessed with autism and encourages women to love themselves. Learn more about Pat at **www.MeetOurAuthors.com.**

From Corner to Corner

Marissa Nicole Shaw

"People are fascinated by robots because they're machines that can mimic life." ~Colin Angle

My possessor took me out of the box, plugged my body into an electric outlet, and I came alive. I am a robot vacuum cleaner. I have permission to meander around a human household on an assignment to suck up dirt and debris.

A lot of people love me and my fellow robots. However, I could get on the nerves of some. My suggestion for individuals interested in purchasing a fellow robot is that they baby-proof their home before the first use regardless of whether they have children.

The first day on the job, in a space I hadn't learned yet, I ran over and almost ate several wires and got caught up in a Mylar balloon with a long string. I stopped mid-mission. I flashed my lights as a signal for help. The mortal then turned me over and untangled me. My electrical circuits were safe from harm.

With each purchase, a person and robot enter into a partnership. We both have our specific roles. I must clean floors while the human makes sure to empty my dustbin and keep me running efficiently. Every commitment is different but is no less important.

Marissa Nicole Shaw lives with her vacuum, Wallie. Find out how to reach Marissa at **www.MeetOurAuthors.com.**

Sandy Toes

Katie De Souza

"Every day is a new beginning." ~*Katie De Souza*

Walking barefoot along the sandy beach, I love watching the waves roll in and break against the shore. A light sea breeze blows gently through my hair as I deeply breathe in and exhale out the salty air. I love starting my day connecting with nature and being outside in the fresh air. I am joined by my beautiful furry friend, little Guarana, my bulldog, who enjoys exploring the sand and digging little holes.

Having some time in the morning to exercise gives me more energy for the day ahead. I am able to think about what I would like to achieve and create a clear vision for the day, which enables me to be more productive. As I absorb the early morning sun rays, lots of ideas come to me, and answers to my questions become clear. I can see opportunities where there were once obstacles, and my mind becomes more laser-focused on what I want.

I am very lucky to live near a beach to be able to enjoy daily moments like these with my four-legged friend.

Katie De Souza is an author and life coach who helps people start their own business turning their passion into profits and leading a happy and healthy life. Learn more about Katie at **www.MeetOurAuthors.com.**

Celebrating a Gazillion Little Things

Nancy J. Haberstich

"If you don't like bacteria, you're on the wrong planet."
~Stewart Brand

I have a gazillion little things living inside my body that keep me healthy. So do you. They are bacteria, and a gazillion might be a conservative estimate. There is a common misconception that all bacteria produce disease and should be avoided.

Did you know there are almost three pounds of bacteria inside the human body that work undercover to support mental and physical health? They were a gift from mother and the environment at your birth. This community of bacteria is called the human microbiome. Most of these microscopic assets live in the gut and feed on insoluble fiber. They help us digest food, create essential vitamins, bolster our immune system, improve our moods and fight off some invading pathogenic bacteria. A thriving microbiome is dependent upon balance, diversity and numbers.

Your responsibility is to feed them prebiotic foods like raw asparagus and add diversity to the population with fermented vegetables like sauerkraut. You should avoid processed food and unnecessary antibiotics since these will deplete their numbers.

Though it might seem strange to celebrate a community of little probiotic bacteria hiding in your gut, the microbiome is a real asset to your health. Celebrate the microscopic things in life.

Nancy J. Haberstich is a specialist in "little things." She teaches practical microbiology and infection prevention to people of all ages with the help of nanobugs®. Learn more at **www.MeetOurAuthors.com.**

Awareness Revisited

Amy Kelsall

"Little things coming together create a truly blessed life. A smattering of little things create a larger picture for celebration each day." ~Amy Kelsall

Watching my dogs as they watch me feed them each morning—twirling body language, bright and perky eyes and ears and happy sounds all around.

Watering my plants with special care, encouraging them to not develop or drop yellow leaves, to stand up tall and grow strong each day.

Gazing into my horse's deep brown eyes for three to five minutes a day is truly magical, mesmerizing and meditative. It connects us in a special way that he has come to expect and know.

It is special to look closely at pussy willows, which complement the texture, color and softness of my living room, while wondering how, why, when and from what they originated.

Hearing the purr of my 28-year-old classic four-wheel-drive car engine as it starts right up, ready to go on an adventure like old times. Covering myself with my furry black, white and brown cowhide while snuggling into my cushy couch is a treat. With hot cider in hand, I am ready to watch the next episode of "Heartland."

I am so grateful for these fleeting yet conscious moments. They are mini adventures that keep me grounded and appreciative of all in the world.

Find out more about Amy Kelsall at **www.MeetOurAuthors.com.**

A Truly Magical Garden

Anne Hunter Logue

"To plant a garden is to believe in tomorrow." ~*Audrey Hepburn*

I have always loved gardens even as a child. Growing up reading *The Secret Garden* and imagining a secret place to daydream and create my fantasy world was so intriguing to me. *Alice in Wonderland* also took place in a garden. Remember the whimsical tea party with the Mad Hatter and the Cheshire cat?

I think of my garden as painting with flowers of different colors and textures, and each year my palette changes and my garden transforms and grows. Expansive and beautifully curated gardens and such a treat to visit and enjoy, like Monet's garden that was the inspiration for his paintings.

My favorite garden story, however, is about a man living in New York City who decided to plant a garden in the tiny strip of land between the street and the sidewalk. He had to clear away the beer cans and the cigarette butts, and the City gave him many citations because that area is city property, but he persisted. The garden grew and he brought kids into the project and taught them about sustainable gardens and how to grow vegetables even in the most challenging of places and circumstances. As Lady Bird Johnson said, "Where flowers bloom, so does hope."

Anne Hunter Logue is a healing practitioner and children's author of The *Story of the Sun* and *I Once Had a Tiger*. Learn more about Anne at **www.MeetOurAuthors.com.**

Topanga and Cujo

Theresa Scandale

"Such short little lives our pets have to spend with us, and they spend most of it waiting for us to come home each day."
~John Grogan

The little things I'm most grateful for come in furry little packages—one seven pounds and the other 15.

Topanga arrived in 2013. From the moment she saw me, she knew we were perfect together. While her siblings were exploring my living room, she immediately jumped on my lap and started licking my face. To be truthful, I originally chose her sister. It wasn't until they were almost out the door that I shouted to the owner, "Wait! I changed my mind!" And thank goodness I did because I cannot imagine my life without her.

We have been on countless journeys together—across the country, across the ocean, across Spain. She is the cuddliest furball I've ever known, and I'm grateful every day that she's mine.

Cujo is new to the family, but I love him just the same. He's quite vocal about what he wants. I'm told he even chose his own name. As stubborn as he can be, he is just as loving, affectionate and protective of me.

I go to sleep with them by my side, and I wake up to them staring at me, waiting for me to start the day! When I'm petting one, I can feel another little pair of eyes staring at me wondering, "When's it my turn?" I think I'm getting the hang of distributing my affection equally. No matter what kind of day I'm having, they always show me unconditional love.

And that's more than I can say for most humans.

Theresa Scandale is a writer, teacher of English as a foreign language (EFL), aspiring linguist and genealogy enthusiast. She travels with her dog Topanga and runs a blog and YouTube channel. Learn more about Theresa at **www.MeetOurAuthors.com.**

Mom's Chicken Soup

Donna Kozik

"The most important thing is, even if we're apart, I'll always be with you." ~A.A. Milne

Six magical ingredients: chicken, carrots, celery, parsley, salt and water. Put them together, simmer for an hour or so and it's like a time machine taking me back to the farm I grew up on near Union City, PA.

Mom made this soup for years on the GE electric stove, and we ate bowl after bowl sitting on the living room couch in front of the TV. It was a sought-after specialty when we had colds because isn't that what the doctor ordered?

Back then there was one more ingredient that doesn't fit in with my low-carb lifestyle but I still remember fondly: kluski! These wide egg noodles with the Polish name were dropped into the bottom of a deep bowl with the steaming soup poured over them. My mouth waters now thinking of it.

During 2020, I frequently turned to this homemade recipe to bring a sense of comfort to evenings spent alone watching too much news. It was good to have a bit of Mom there with me—her memory alive in my mind as I slurped my magical chicken soup.

Donna Kozik is a *USA Today* and *Wall Street Journal* best-selling author with a passion for getting people published. Find out more at **www.MeetOurAuthors.com**.

What We Look Forward To

Editor's Note: As we go to press in June 2021, the United States and parts of the world are starting to come out of the year-long pandemic. I asked contributors to this edition of The Community Book Project to give me a "one liner" about what they most look forward to doing again.

Here are their responses. And let us never take the little things for granted again.

Tammy Atchley
...hugging and being close to family and friends.
...breathing fresh air while shopping.

Brenda Lynn Nielsen
...singing with my choir.
...intimate brunches and dinner parties with great food, wine and stimulating conversations.

Linda Luhman
...to be rid of the feeling of shouting when I'm speaking with a mask on.
...being able to resume community fundraising activities. Organizations miss interacting with their supporters!

Emma Elizabeth Robinson
...meeting people again.
...my dream job.

Lauren Julia Robinson
...seeing friends.
...seeing family.

Mary Ammon MacNeith
...kissing and hugging my mom, who turns 92 this year.
...seeing my newborn grandkids and my one-year-old grandnephew for the first time in person.

Shirley E. Kennedy
...rediscovering and cherishing the many blessings in my life.
...relishing opportunities to share love and good times with all my family together again in safety.

Ginny Lang
...big, beautiful tomatoes that taste like summer when they're fresh and then make the tastiest sauce for winter lasagna.
...rereading all my Charles de Lint books—my favorite magical urban fantasy writer.

Sarah-Jane Watson
...enjoying a cup of coffee and conversation with friends.
...going to the library with my niece and nephew for the first time.

Sharon G. Teed
...being able to see my grandchildren.
...feeling the freedom to come and go as I please.

Chineme Noke
...attending the sauna and steam rooms again after lockdown.
...being able to travel freely after lockdown.

Roberta Gold
...hugging my friends, family and special people in my life.
...feeling comfortable around others I may not know so well.

Kathy Carpenter
...finding the sparkle out in the world.
...being able to enjoy live theatre once more, especially musicals.

Melissa Rowe
...traveling anywhere in the world.
...the pleasure of giving and receiving big hugs.

Joan Powell
...celebrating my 10th wedding anniversary (which was in 2020).
...having fun without fear!

Alberta Cotner
...all the beautiful flowers that come throughout the warmer months.
...the different writing workshops and celebrations with associates, friends and family.

Bonita Joy Yoder
...hugs with friends.
...improv shows.

Karen Lynn Robinson
...dinners out with friends.
...traveling!

Tracey Doctor
...my very first cruise experience.
...a luxury spa day with my daughter.

Julaina Kleist-Corwin
...publishing my book called *My Mother's Cancer—What Worked and What Didn't.*
...more new attendees in my writing courses.

Dena Crecy
...monthly lunch and play at Jubilee Theatre with girlfriends.
...outdoor activities with three grandchildren.

Cynde Canepa
...undivided conversations with my husband at our favorite restaurant.
...going out to restaurants with family and friends.

Carol A. Peña
...tight hugs and butterfly kisses from my 90-year-old mom.
...the noisy sounds and smell of fresh popcorn in a movie theater.

Carole A MacLean

...seeing the smile of my beautiful and creative 27-going-on-40-year-old daughter in person rather than on Zoom for the first time in 18 months and being in her space so we can bake cookies, talk about life and giggle about everything and anything.

...traveling freely about this incredible country, the good old United States of America in cars, trains and planes without the fear of an invisible enemy lurking around every corner.

Kathy Carpenter

...being seen and seeing all the beautiful faces surrounding us as we go about our lives out in the world.

Cindy Barnard Mills

...hugging my grandkids mask free!

...Saturday breakfast with my brothers at our favorite restaurant.

Moira Shepard

...going for a scrumptious high tea with my girlfriends at Tea Rose Garden in Pasadena.

...finally seeing "Hamilton" live with Aunt Marguerite.

Holly Pitas

...having dinner with friends in a lively, crowded restaurant.

...having my face free of a mask.

Diane Rasmussen Lovitt

...seeing and hugging family members that I have missed for over a year.

...attending a live music performance.

Linda Lou Lilyquist

...walking down the aisles at Costco and enjoying "lunchtime" samples.

...seeing everyone's entire smiling face—sans masks!

Get Your Free Gratitude Journal!

Keep a daily record of life's positive moments (big and small) with this printable gratitude journal that has room for reflecting on all the things that make your life a blessing.

- Take 60 seconds to shine a light on what's good!
- Affirmations and inspirational quotes to lift you up.
- Delivered via a colorful PDF printable.

Pick up your free gratitude journal!

www.TheGratitudeJournalProject.com

Made in the USA
Las Vegas, NV
13 July 2021